enemies (EH neh meez)—Animals that try to kill or hurt other animals.

thaw—To change from frozen to liquid.

WEIRD ANIMAL HOMES

Some termites build big nests above the ground. Some birds live all the way at the top of Mount Everest! Life is not easy for many animals. Let's read about the weird places they live, and how they stay alive!

A termite mound can be as tall as a tree.

ANTARCTIC SHRIMP

It's dark and cold down here!

Scientists thought that nothing lived deep under the Antarctic ice. They drilled a hole through 600 FEET of ice and sent down a camera. Imagine their surprise! A shrimp swam by in the dark, freezing water!

It's weird, but it's true!

CAVE SALAMANDER
Who turned out the lights?

Some salamanders have NO eyes. Even if they had eyes, they wouldn't be able to see. These salamanders live deep in caves where there is no light. They stopped growing eyes because they did not need them.

It's weird, but it's true!

EASTERN WOOD FROG
This frog turns to ice!

Some frogs can live in the icy cold. The eastern wood frog turns to ice in the winter! First its eyeballs freeze. Then the frog stops breathing. Its heart stops beating. At last spring comes. The frog **thaws** and hops away.

It's weird, but it's true!

CACTUS WREN
Stay away from my babies!

Snakes, hawks, and owls like to eat baby birds. A cactus wren is pretty tricky. She builds her nest in a cactus plant. The sharp thorns of the plant keep **enemies** away from her eggs and babies.

It's weird, but it's true!

Deep Sea Anglerfish

Here fishy, fishy, fishy . . .

In the deepest, darkest part of the ocean, a fish swims by. It looks scary! It has a part that looks like a fishing pole growing out of its head. On the end is a glowing light. Little fish swim up to get a closer look. GULP! Lunch for the anglerfish.

It's weird, but it's true!

These jets of hot wat[er] are sometimes called black smokers.

Black Smoker Tube Worms

What a big hot tub!

Tube Worms

Jets of hot water shoot out of cracks at the bottom of the deep sea. Giant tube worms grow near the jets. They do not have mouths or stomachs or any way to poop. The worms soak up everything they need to live from the hot water. That's their food.

It's weird, but it's true!

Naked Mole Rats

A mouth full of dirt

Naked mole rats live in deep, dark tunnels.
The rats do not need to see, so they are almost blind.
The tunnels stay warm, so the rats do not need fur.
They do need great big teeth—for digging.

It's weird, but it's true!

MOUNT EVEREST CHOUGH
Oh boy, snacks!

Mount Everest is the highest mountain in the world. People climb and climb to try to get to the top. Flocks of birds are already up there! They fly around the climbers. They are called choughs (CHUFFS). The choughs eat food left at the camps. It is an easy meal for them.

It's weird, but it's true!

LEARN MORE

Books

Barnhill, Kelly Regan. *Animals With No Eyes*. Mankato, Minn.: Capstone Press, 2008.

Gray, Susan. *Walking Catfish*. Ann Arbor, Mich.: Cherry Lake Publishing, 2008.

Pipe, Jim. *Scary Creatures of the Deep*. Danbury, Conn.: Franklin Watts, 2009.

Weber, Valerie. *Giant Tubeworms*. Milwaukee: Gareth Stevens Publishing, 2005.

LEARN MORE

Web Sites

Animal Planet
http://animal.discovery.com/videos/corwins-quest-
mangrove-mudskipper.html

National Geographic
http://animals.nationalgeographic.com/animals/fish/
anglerfish.html

INDEX

To our wonderful grandchildren: Andrew, Charlie, Kate, and Caroline

Enslow Elementary, an imprint of Enslow Publishers, Inc.

Enslow Elementary® is a registered trademark of Enslow Publishers, Inc.

Copyright © 2012 by Carmen Bredeson

Library of Congress Cataloging-in-Publication Data

Bredeson, Carmen.
  Weird but true animal homes / Carmen Bredeson.
    p. cm. — (Weird but true science)
  Includes index.
   ISBN 978-0-7660-3861-5
  1. Habitat (Ecology)—Juvenile literature. I. Title.
  QH541.14.B74 2011
  591.56′4—dc22
                         2010035876

Paperback ISBN: 978-1-59845-368-3

Printed in China

052011 Leo Paper Group, Heshan City, Guangdong, China

10 9 8 7 6 5 4 3 2 1

To Our Readers: We have done our best to make sure all Internet Addresses in this book were active and appropriate when we went to press. However, the author and the publisher have no control over and assume no liability for the material available on those Internet sites or on other Web sites they may link to. Any comments or suggestions can be sent by e-mail to comments@enslow.com or to the address on the back cover.

Photo Credits: Alamy: © John Norman, p. 21, © tbkmedia.de, p. 13; © Frans Lanting, pp. 1, 19; Minden Pictures: © David Shale/npl, p. 15; © Ingo Arndt, p. 7, © Tony Heald/npl, p. 3 (top); naturepl.com: © David Kjaer, pp. 2, 12, © Visuals Unlimited, p. 8; Photo Researchers, Inc.: British Antarctic Survey, p. 6, Science Source, pp. 16, 17; Shutterstock.com, pp. 3 (bottom), 4, 11.

Cover Photo: © Frans Lanting

Note to Parents and Teachers: The *Weird But True Science* series supports the National Science Education Standards for K–4 science. The Words to Know section introduces subject-specific vocabulary words, including pronunciation and definitions. Early readers may need help with these new words.

Enslow Elementary
an imprint of
Enslow Publishers, Inc.
40 Industrial Road
Box 398
Berkeley Heights, NJ 07922
USA
http://www.enslow.com

CONTENTS

WEIRD BUT TRUE SCIENCE

Weird But True Animal Homes

Series Science Consultant:
Mary Poulson, PhD
Central Washington University
Ellensburg, WA

Series Literacy Consultant:
Allan A. De Fina, PhD
Dean, College of Education/Professor of Literacy Education
New Jersey City University
Past President of the New Jersey Reading Association

Carmen Bredeson